Musings Of A Man With Nothing Left To Lose

IN MEMORY OF:

Philip Tewel
Tony Gray
George Unsworth
Cathy Carpenter
Chris Petelle
Bill Colegrove
Terri Strahley
Tom Cox
Jeff Hendricks
Willie Wright
Brian Abel
Brian Sullivan

And all others who left us way too soon.
Sadly missed but always kept close to our hearts.

Musings Of A Man With Nothing Left To Lose

Introduction:

I was actually surprised, after my recent battle with cancer, that I had anything at all left to write about.

Once you've been through cancer – and are still going through chemotherapy – one would think you might just be tapped out for now.

But, not *me*.

Not this tough old bird, not a true *survivor*.

I've got *plenty* left to say.

Except this time, I will be looking *backward* in time instead of forward. I already have a pretty good idea where my future may lead me, so let's look back on *how* I got here, shall we?

It should be an interesting trip to say the least, because I've lived a *very* interesting life.

The good times, the bad, and the in between.

But, do me favor, okay? When we finally reach the end of my journey, don't stand in judgement of me uness you've walked a mile in my shoes.

In all honesty? I don't think that a lot of you would have survived my life, and still come out a better person for it – and believe me, it wasn *not* an easy road to success.

There is a song by Billy Joel entitled, "Only The Good Die Young." I tend to disagree with that, because this old man is still here.

For better or worse, I'm not sure yet, but I'm sure of one thing; by the time we reach the end, I'm quite sure that you will have lived a lifetime right along with me, and will be amazed by it all.

So...let us begin the journey, shall we?

David Boyer / March 9th, 2024

Part One

I'll begin by a brief examination of my early years, which, much later down the road, helped to form my later years in terms of my so called, "development," as a human being.

Some of us develop sooner than others, in terms of maturity, intelligence, etc., then some of us, like yours truly, go kicking and screaming into adulthood like a human tornado, tossing all caution – and any sense of normalcy – to the wind.

Why, you ask, would I do so? I haven't figured that out yet, but maybe by the end of this story, I will.

#

I had a good childhood, actually.

I was raised by two God fearing, hard working, loving parents, who only wanted the best for me, so I didn't have much of an excuse for the way I ended up as a teenager.

Yeah, I know; there are the typical excuses, like peer pressure, running with the wrong crowd, etc., but considering my idyllic childhood, it must have been a choice I made on my own.

But...why?

I guess we'll find out soon enough.

In all honesty? I sincerely believe now that God, in all his infinite love and wisdom, does have a plan for all of us, whether we understand it at the time or not, and his plan for us, even in the worst of times, happens for a specific reason.

In my case? I guess God left the flood gates wide open, and knew that someday, somehow, it would be for the betterment of myself, both spiritually and otherwise.

What other reason could there be?

So...onward we go!

Part Two

First stop, my teenage years.

Whereas most teenagers in my home were out riding bikes or playing at the local parks or taking interest in some type of normal activities that were common for the 1970s, I, myself, was still lying in bed, too tired from sneaking out late at night to wake up at a normal hour.

I was almost like a recluse, a hermit, opting to sleep late and only stirring from my slumber to eat or go to the bathroom or take a bath.

It was like my bedroom was my *hiding place.* But, hiding from *what?*

That was the question.

As I grew into my teenage years, from the age of thirteen to eighteen years old, it was like I was living in my own little world, one of 70s rock music and TV shows and spending time with my equally non-ambitious, slacker buddies.

I know that could apply to a lot of folks out there who weren't necessarily the slacker type, but, in my case, I took it to extremes.

#

I was what you might call a "nocturnal" teenager, in my every day habits.

I would either tell my parents I was spending the night at a friend's house, or just sneak out after my parents were asleep { I had a key to the back door} and I would run the streets all night until dawn, trying to find someone to hang out with, or, as I would do more often than not, wing it solo.

Not that I didn't appreciate my friend's company, mind you, but some odd reason, being alone, for me, at times was almost theraputic, I guess you could say.

That and partaking in some cheap alcohol, and not having to share it with anyone.

I had a fake ID back then, and looked older than I was, so I would use the ID at the local package store before they closed for the night, grab a half pint of some type of cheap liquor { normally vodka} and then hit the streets, in search of whatever I might find out there.

Whatever it was I had been looking for, I had apparently never found it, because here I am today, the better for not having found it, and knowing now *why* I didn't find it.

I know that most likely doesn't make any sense to you, but now, it does for me.

Let us move on.

Part Three

As I entered my adult years, between the ages of 18 and 21, my normal routine was temporarily interrupted by that crazy thing called *life*.

Growing up.

Being a *responsible* adult.

I did pretty well at first. My parents gave a me a job at their local dry cleaning-laundry business, and there for a while, spending my days working hard and my nights relaxing in front of the TV, I had become a "responsible" adult.

For a *while*, as I said.

After the first year or so, working eight or ten hours days over a hot press and my nights just doing my best to recuperate, I began to to become disillusioned with it all, and began slowly but surely, to withdraw into my own little world again.

Imagine that.

#

It wasn't that I was lazy, mind you.

I was still young and healthy and full of life and always ready to make a buck and earn a living. For me, it was the fact that the longer I strayed *away* from my own little world, the more I longed to retreat back into it.

So I did.

#

The transition was slow at first, but quickly picked up momentum as I got back into my old habits, the main one of course being partaking in the demon alcohol.

That's what it felt like to me back then; as if some evil little demon had invaded my body – and my mind – and was bound and determined, hell or high water, to ruin my life.

Or at least the best years of it, anyway.

My youth.

I had become a "functioning" alcoholic.

Sadly, I would remain that way for the next twenty-five years.

Thus began the long, hard, seemingly endless journey back to where I belonged all along.

A sick old man with wonderous and eye opening musings to share with the world.

Part Four

The musings.

A reflection of thought.

I have so many to share, too. Some of them happy, some sad, but *all* of them pertaining to my *very* interesting life journey.

Like today, for example.

This morning, my mind wanders back to the day I found out that I had cancer – October 13th, 2023.

The day my life changed forever.

Yes, I know that I left a big empty space in here, but I'm not nearly finished with my *musings* just yet.

#

That day was so terrifying, so gut wrenching.

But that day was the day that opened my eyes to my musings, my reflections, of where I was supposed to be all along at the *end* of my journey.

As I sit here today, for example, I am thinking about my sweet mother, who sadly passed away two years ago. I think of the years I took care of her before she was placed in a nursing home. I think of the guilt and pain I felt that day, having to make such a decision.

Yet I also think back on my youth, so lost long ago, but happy days in between, like my days as a little kid, when Mom and me would spend a Saturday morning in the kitchen, making her famous peanut butter cookies.

I know a lot of guys out there think that cooking and baking is supposed to be a woman's job in the kitchen, but I, myself, have always enjoyed it.

Back in those days, it was all made from *scratch*, too. Flour, sugar, baking soda, baking powder, eggs, peanut butter, vanilla extract, all of it mixed up from scratch and baked up fresh in the oven.

One of the main things I remember about the days we were baking was the *smell* coming from the kitchen, too. Well, I wouldn't call it a smell, more than an *aroma* of stuff baking in the kitchen. There was absolutely nothing like the aroma of cookies baking in the kitchen, and the anticipation of getting to eat a cookie fresh out of the oven with a big glass of ice cold milk.

By the time we were done, the kitchen would be a big mess, but I was more than glad to help clean it up if it meant getting to nibble on those tasty cookies for the next few days.

Yes...*happy* musings, indeed.

But they would be forgotten soon enough, for decades, in fact.

On with the journey...

Part Five

The odd thing about my reflections these days is, they come in dribs and drabs, like a leaky water spicket, or, they come flooding in like a dam has burst.

Either way, they come, for better or worse.

Although these days, it's mostly for the better.

Just like this morning, when I was thinking back on my youth again – and just how many friends I've sadly lost over the years.

Yes, I know, that's a *negative* reflection, but, at times, a negative thought can lead you to a more positive thought in the end.

For example, an old friend of mine, Tony, whom I'd known for over forty years, passed away recently. I didn't even get to attend his fineral service, because I was at the hospital that day, getting ready to go through another 96 hour round of chemo.

Aggressive chemo.

Afterward, I felt so sad – and guilty – about not attending his funeral, but, as the days passed by, I realized that he wouldn't have wanted to me to feel guilty over it. Or sad.

He would want me to be happy for him; he was no longer sick or suffering, and he would want me to be glad for him, and just remember the good times way back when.

So...that's exactly what I did.

I felt much better afterward.

\#

I also firmly believe that it was alos part of God's plan for me, going through sad times but remembering the good ones, to show me that a person always has to take the bad with the good, to make us a *stronger* person, a true *survivor.*

Just like everything I'd been going through lately – the cancer, the chemo, and it's terrible side effects – has slowly but surely made me not only a better man, but a stronger one as well.

What more could a man in my postion ask for?

So...I move on.

Part Six

Today, I am sitting here typing away as the *musings* come flooding back in again, like a waterfall.

The 1960s was actually a banner decade for myself – and a lot of other kids my age.

Life was so much more simple then, and kids actually had some respect, some morals that had been instilled in them by their parents.

I'm not saying that kids that grew up in the baby boomer era were perfect by any mens, but, it's just plain fact that our generation was, by far, a lot easier to make happy – and at the same time, keep under control.

Many years before the age of the internet and social networking and designer clothes and designer drugs and cheap alcohol and tattoo sleeves and multiple body piercings and music that would make a baby boomer want to jump out of a moving car, life was so much easier, less complicated – and less dangerous.

#

Nobody worked on Sundays – we were all in Church.

We were raised on the Bible and believing in God and Jesus Christ.

We were taught respect and manners and saying thank you and you're welcome.

We did our daily chores and worked for our

spending money.

We never talked back to our parents, and if we had, it would have resulted in a butt whooping we'd never forget.

And through it all, we were still happy, stable kids who were thankful for what we had.

Some of my most memorable moments of the 1960s were:

Riding around on my new Stingray bike and chasing the mosquito truck.

Mom taking me to the old Rainbow Beach.

My first kiss, from a pretty little girl who had a crush on me in First grade.

Walking down to the old Dairy Queen on Vigo Street for a Dilly Bar or a milkshake.

Walking down to Larry Mouzin's barber shop on 10th Street for a haircut on Saturday mornings.

Going to the old New Moon Theater one Halloween night to watch a double feature – hosted by Sammy Terry.

Buying my first 45 RPM record, "Born To Be Wild," by Steppenwolf.

My Mom teaching me how to bake her old cookie recipes she had in her Betty Crocker cookbook. {I still have the cookbook, too.}

The first time I mowed the grass by myself.

My Dad taking me golfing with him on a Sunday afternoon at the Elks Club.

Catching fireflies after dark and keeping them in glass jar for a while and then setting them free.

Walking up to the old Tresslar's store for a burger, fries, and a chocolate egg cream, then walking around the store looking at toys and record albums.

Walking down to Lester Square park to ride the famous "butt-burner" slide to impress the neighborhood girls.

Hanging out with my buddies on weekends and finding all sorts of {harmless} mischief to get ourselves into.

Walking up to the George Rogers Clark Memorial to sit on the river wall and watch the sunsets.

Sitting in the living room watching family friendly TV shows with my brother and my parents, without fear of seeing anything "questionable" on the TV screen.

Digging up worms in my back yard, to use for fishing bait.

Eating one of those worms on a dare just to gross out my buddies.

My third grade teacher telling my Mom I should pursue a career in writing.

My first pet, a black cat named Lady, whom would patiently wait for me in the living room window every day after school.

Walking down to the Wabash River on the 4th of July to watch the fireworks.

Making Chef Boyar Dee pizza mixes with my Mom on Saturday afternoons and watching cartoons.

Yep...I think the 1960s was a banner decade for kids my age to grow up in.

Yes...the 60s were a great time to grow up in, only happy musings there.

But life goes on.

Part Seven

Today, as I sit here wating for another flood of musings, all I get is a trickle.

Drip...drip...*drip*.

What little that does come to me is unhappy and embarrassing, to say the least.

Gotta take the bad with the good.

Yes, I know.

#

In the 70s, I was already acting like I had nothing left to lose.

The 1970s came rolling in with a big bang, and never looked back.

Whether it be music or clothing styles or hair styles or just 70s pop culture in general, it was a wild time in my life, looking around in awe at how just a few years could make such a difference.

By the early 70s, when I entered JR high school, my whole appearance – and my attitude – to a certain extent, had changed dramatically.

That's when I was first introduced to the demon alcohol.

Gone were the dress chinos and corduroy slacks and had been replaced with the latest style in blue jeans. Gone were the Sunday dress shoes and casual penny loafers, and had been replaced with the latest style in tennis shoes, my personal preference being either *Pro Keds* or *Converse*.

Add a somewhat longer hair style, a tye-dyed t-shirt, and an old Army jacket, and...*voila!*

Mr Cool.

Mr Groovy.

Or, Mr dumbass, depending on how you looked at it. I, myself, didn't realize just hoiw dumb I was acting until it was almost too late.

Despite my obvious rebellious attitude, deep down, I was still the same old me – just wrapped up in a somewhat "updated" package.

Underneath all of the "coolness," I was still the nice young man who went to church and obeyed his parents and wanted them to be proud of me.

But at the times when I allowed the demon alcohol to take me over, and became the oddball reclusive hermit once again, I was like Dr Jekyll and Mr Hyde.

But that's a whole other story altogether. Please allow me to move past it, and share the *good* musings for a moment...

#

Going to the *new* Rainbow Beach to hang out and talk with the pretty girls. I would spend the summer at the city beach with my similarly disinterested friends, smoking cigarettes, guzzling Mountain Dew, and bantering with (ogling) the local girls kind enough to model the latest JC Penney swimwear. It doesn't take much to make a seventeen year old boy happy.

Riding around in my friend Tony's new Chevy van, listening to "Running On Empty" by Jackson Browne, and letting the cool summer breeze blow through our hair.

Hanging out at the infamous "Alice," across the street from Clark Jr High, smoking cigarettes and trying to look tough, until someone tougher than me gave me a royal butt-whooping.

Going to the old New Moon theater to see movies like *The Planet of the Apes* and *The Omen*. I can remember watching *The Exorcist* there in 1973, and I couldn't sleep for a week.

Hanging out at Gregg Park playing Frisbee, washing and waxing my friend's cars, and listening to the top ten hits on the local radio station.

Hanging out at Creole Lanes playing pool and listening to the jukebox and playing pinball.

Cruising Sixth Street on Friday and Saturday nights, and cruising through the Burger Chef parking lot, then on to Frost Top and Putt Putt Golf.

Attending school sponsored dances with live bands at the Adams Coliseum.

Going to the Airport Pits in Illinois to swim and ride all terrain vehicles and party a little bit.

Attending a school sponsored Halloween costume party dance dressed up as the rock band KISS, and winning first prize.

Going to the Italian Village pizza house on Second Street on Sundays to eat pizza and play Space Invaders.

Just...having some simple and harmless fun.

Then...the 1980s kicked in, and introduced us all to a whole new way of life all over again.

And a lot of new ways for me to create even more musings to look back on now.

Bad with the good.

Always remember that.

It is what led you here, and now.

Yes, I know.

Part Eight

Today, I woke up feeling very weak again.

Yesterday, I was bleeding from my mouth and nasal passages – yet another wonderful side effect of the chemo – but today, the bleeding has stopped altogether, but has left me feeling weak and drained of any energy.

The bad with the good.

Gotta hang in there!

So far, no happy musings today.

#

Today, as I sit here typing away again, my mind has finally opened up again, and I am seeing reflections of my own mortality, more than anything else.

I mean, much more today than usual, like my mind is a dam, and I just pulled a switch and opened the flood gates on purpose, and I'm drowning in the flood, too many memories at once.

Suddenly, the images in my mind stop abrubtly, like a switch has been flicked again, and all I see is more *recent* images, then back again.

I'm sick. I'm healed. I'm sick again. I'm in remission. I'm sick again.

And here comes good old Mr Chemo, my constant companion, who is worse than any amount of the demon alcohol ever.

Hey, dumbass! It's me, Mr Chemo. You know you don't have to just sit here and suffer, right? The liquor store is only a twenty minute walk from your house, remember? Just saying.

No thanks, my mind says. *One little demon is quite enough for now.*

Then again, as I've said before, this is just yet another day of reflection, the kind of days I'm becoming quite used to these days, and nothing more.

Your eyes have to be *open* to see the light at the end of the proverbial tunnel. And your mind.

Your very heart and soul.

If you don't, you won't be able to find that pot of gold waiting for you at the end of the proverbial rainbow.

The pot of musings. The ones that will eventually lead you back *home*. To the place where you will finally understand *why* you are here, and were *meant* to still be here all along.

The *end* of my journey.

But I'm not quite there yet.

Part Nine

Today, my mind suddenly drifted back to New Year's Eve, the year 1983.

For what reason I wasn't sure at first, that is, until another *musing* kicked in, and I could see the reflection of a woman I had a massive crush on in highschool.

Debbie.

I had met up with her for the first time through a mutual friend, and I was instantly smitten with her – what my mother would have referred to as "an infatuation" - but it felt real to me.

But as always, as we grow older, graduate and move on into adulthood, we all eventually lose contact at least to a certain exent, and I didn't see her again until that night in 1983.

A close friend of mine, George {who sadly passed away in 2018 } and I had decided to have a keg party, and had invited all of our friends from school.

As the night moved on, and our guests began to arrive, lo and behold, there was Debbie, as beautiful and bright eyed as ever, strolling in the door – alone.

No date in sight.

I knew then I had to make my move, before it was too late.

But as the night went on, I had realized that was my biggest mistake.

It happened a lot in one's youth, friends and girlfriends both coming and going as routinely as one would brush their teeth or drink their morning coffee.

Young love – or infatuation, as my mother would have called it – was just part of growing up back in those days and done so much more innocently than the generations that followed my own. But the hurt, the genuine heartache was still there just the same, and especially when the object of your affections doesn't feel the same way.

That's what happened with Debbie.

Don't get me wrong; we enjoyed chatting and catching up and having a good time in general, but once midnight rolled around – and the obligatory New Years Eve kisses began – and I took Debbie in my arms and welcomed her warm embrace, and kissed those sweet little lips {they tasted like peaches} I think I fell head over heels for her at that moment.

But it wasn't meant to be.

As the night faded away and the morning rolled around and the crowd thinned out, the only two people left were Debbie and I, sitting on the couch, and talking about my feelings for her.

Needless to say, she didn't feel the same way.

#

Point being, now that I look back on that night so long ago, I realize now that it was *meant* to be.

Yet another disappointment, another heartache, which much later – around forty-one years later, to be exact – would prove to be yet another example of why I ended up where I am now, and how it made me a better and stronger man for it.

It seemed with each new "musing," each new reflection of my past, it was always something that had played a *pivotal* role in my life, one of understanding and having learned life's lessons the *hard* way, the *best* way, and not to make the same mistakes again.

Begin living in *reality*.

It's fine to hope and daydream, but you have to know when to separate reality from fantasy, and move on.

So that's what I did – and now, all these years later, I am a better man for it all.

Part Ten

It's really funny isn't it – or ironic, actually – how we spend most of our lives, the part that is supposed to be the *best* part of our lives, going through so much unhappiness and uncertainty, only to reach the final plateau, which can be nothing more than a place of loneliness and despair?

It doesn't have to be that way, no, but at times you can't help but wonder if it was all really worth it.

Just like with chemotherapy, it all comes with the territory.

What I mean is, just like the chemo comes with so many unpleasant side effects, life in general can be the same. You spend so many years learning life's hard lessons and just when you think you've reached your so called "golden years," it all seems to quickly and cruelly evaporate into thin air right before your very eyes.

I still wake up some mornings, to this day, sort of confused and even frightened by it all.

I do understand, yet, I don't understand.

It's a very weird feeling, to say the least.

But, as always, I just accept it for what it is, and move on, hoping that what's left of my golden years won't be spent suffering with more cancer or, worse yet, do it alone and uncertain.

God is always there, though, and I'm sure he will make all of this clearly apparent to me in the end.

I just hope I can make him proud of me in the meantime, and when it is time for me to leave this world, I can do so with some dignity and grace.

I hope.

Amen.

Part Eleven

So...I move on – again.

Today is yet another day – the sun is shining, the birds are singing, and it's so far a good day.

I feel weak and tired again – the side effects of the chemo seem to never lay dormant for too long – but otherwise, I feel hopeful it will be a good day.

Sometimes, that's all you have left; *hope*.

Today, I'm hoping that I will be able to eat and swallow food without too much pain or discomfort, and drink water without choking on it. Like I've said before, some days you have to take the bad with the good, and if that involves considering being able to do something as simple as eating normally as a giant blessing, then so be it.

Each day on this Earth, that I wake up alive and kicking, is a gigantic blessing for me.

The *simple* things.

The things that matter the most, that we all seem to take advantage of until it's too late.

But not any more.

#

To be honest? Eating is the furthest thing from my mind right now, anyway.

I woke up to a much more depressing situation to deal with.

Recently, I had contacted some old friends through Facebook messenger, to let them know of my current state of health, just in case I wouldn't see them again someday, if you get my drift.

These were very *close* friends, mind you – or at least I *thought* they were.

I received no response; not one *I'm sorry*, not one *I hope you get better soon*, nothing.

Don't get me wrong; I'm not saying that anyone *owes* me a response, just because we hung out together, way back when, drinking beer and tossing all caution and responsibility to the wind.

But, you'll have to admit, it is kind of cold for someone you've known for over forty years not to at least say *something* in response.

But there was *nothing*.

But I'll get over it, believe me. Nothing – or nobody – is worth any more tears than I've shed already.

Amen.

Part Twelve

So, as usual, I move on.

Just like I do every day.

Move on to yet another musing of some sort, some reflection of my past – or another depressing vision of my future.

Sit at my computer and type away, adding yet another uncertain chapter to my life story, in hopes that it will, someday, in some way, might benefit others on their own sad journey.

I hope.

#

But today, I will do my best not to focus on the bad things, the *sad* things,

Today, I will move on once again, to yet another musing, another pivotal memory – but this time it will be a *happy* one.

As a matter of fact, I woke up today thinking about how much fun I used to have hanging out at one of my favorite restaurants, Italian Village pizza house.

It was back in the summer of 1979.

Many years before the Big C invaded my body, many years before another heartache, and many years before I had to evaluate my whole existence.

Happy times.

We had a beautiful Summer that year, and my buddies and I would spend the majority of the day at the swimming pits or country cruising, and the majority of our evenings at Italian Village. We even had our own usual "spot," small tables formed in a circle right next to the jukebox and the Space Invaders video game machine.

The food was fantastic – and from a 19-year-old's point of view, eating Stromboli sandwiches and pizza was a lot better than eating your Mom's cooking, which normally consisted of something – God forbid – *healthy* for you. As I look back now, I wish I'd spent a lot more time eating healthy food with my mama, and felt blessed to be able to do so.

But I sure had a good time eating junkfood – along with the other "benefits" of hanging out there.

Like...pretty girls that worked there!

Seriously, though, it was a great place to hang out, and some great people worked there, too.

The night managers, Jim and Carolyn Eakins, were wonderful people, always friendly and fun to be around, and they really enjoyed having our "gang" coming in every night to sit around and eat great food and listen to the jukebox while we planned our evening strategy. They were charmed by our presence there, as we were with theirs.

Looking back now, I sincerely believe that it was my times there that helped to shape me into the man I would become later on, due mainly to the fun, positive atmosphere, a place where I experienced only happy times. A place that showed me that there really *are* happy places out there, that teach us later on, down the road, to try our best to keep a positive attitude, no matter

what life tosses your way.
It sure helped to keep me in a good mood today.
Now, just to get through *tomorrow*.

Part Thirteen

Today...not so good.

This morning, I find myself reflecting back on a time way back in 2003, when I was feeling sort of lonely and depressed, and had decided that it was in my best interest to get drunk – and drive.

Drive to where? It didn't matter, as long as I had my bottle and my cigarettes and a full tank of gas. When you are in that frame of mind – one of deep depression and your brain soaked in cheap vodka – you tend to not make the best decisions.

I can't even remember what I was so sad about – most likely another failed relationship with a woman who shared the same love for living a hopeless and depressing life style – but I climbed in my old Lincoln Towne car, filled it with gas, and hit the road.

If I had known where that road was going to lead me, I would have most definitely stayed home.

#

As I drove down a country road right outside of town, sipping and smoking and listening to the cassette player, blaring the Rolling Stones – *I'll never be, your beast of burden* – thinking I was out of sight from the local police, at least for now, I had floored the car and let the wind blow through my hair and felt so *free*, free from any unpleasant thoughts or memories, at least for a little while, anyway.

That is, until a County Sheriff pulled up behind me, flashing his lights, signaling for me to pull over.

That's the moment my whole life changed, for the next 18 months.

#

Needless to say, I was arrested for a DUI and my driver's license was suspended for six months, and I was placed on supervised probation.

I was *not* a happy camper.

I was so unhappy, in fact, about two months into my probationary period, I had decided to take another country cruise, with my bottle, of course, and edned up having a grand old time.

That is, until I came home, and found out through a phone message that I'd missed a random blood test and I was to report *immediately* to the probation office.

Knowing I had no other choice at the time, I brushed my teeth and headed down to the office – where, shortly thereafter, I was placed under arrest for a probation violation.

That was just the beginning.

#

To make a long story short, I spent the next 14 months – 8 months in jail and 5 months in prison – for my bad choices, and, through it all, I learned yet another valuable life lesson; *NEVER* use alcohol to solve your problems.

It is, at best, merely a *temporary* solution to what could be a *permanent* problem.

Yet another "musing" in my long list of musings, but, one that taught me a very valuable lesson that would eventually lead me to being sober for seventeen years and counting.

Taking the bad with the good, and learning from it; that's what it's all about.

Part Fourteen

And...the musings – and the memories – keep on coming.

Today, it is a cloudy, gloomy, rainy day, which, of course, for a man in my current mental and physical condition, doesn't exactly scream success.

But, as usual, I do my best to hang tough and fight the good fight, mainly because I have no other choice.

I have only ten days before my next chemo treatment, so I have to be prepared, both mentally and physically, to deal with it.

I have also been informed recently that after my chemotherapy is done, I must also begin a short round of a drug called Keytruda, which has the following possible side effects:

Diarrhea (loose stools) or more frequent bowel movements than usual; stools that are black, tarry, sticky, or have blood or mucus; or severe stomach-area (abdomen) pain or tenderness.

Liver problems: yellowing of your skin or the whites of your eyes; severe nausea or vomiting; pain on the right side of your stomach area (abdomen); dark urine (tea colored); or bleeding or bruising more easily than normal.

Hormone gland problems: headaches that will not go away or unusual headaches; eye sensitivity to light; eye problems; rapid heartbeat; increased sweating;

extreme tiredness; weight gain or weight loss; feeling more hungry or thirsty than usual; urinating more often than usual; hair loss; feeling cold; constipation; your voice gets deeper; dizziness or fainting; changes in mood or behavior, such as decreased sex drive, irritability, or forgetfulness.

Kidney problems: decrease in the amount of your urine; blood in your urine; swelling of your ankles; loss of appetite.

Skin problems: rash; itching; skin blistering or peeling; painful sores or ulcers in your mouth or in your nose, throat, or genital area; fever or flu-like symptoms; swollen lymph nodes.

Sounds fun, doesn't it? Not really, but it's apparently something the doctors think I should do to get "better."

So...I move on, and hope for the best.

Part Fifteen

Today is yet another day of reflection.

But this time, of something more pleasant, which is always a good thing.

Today, I woke up thinking about my so called, "fifteen minutes of fame," back in 2011, when, to my utter surprise, I was informed that an on line book publisher, Bear Manor Media, was interested in publishing one of my books.

Little did I know at the time, though, that I would make a lot more money self publishing through Amazon Kindle, but at the time, I felt on top of the world.

The book, a collection of email interviews with well known horror authors, was almost an *instant* success, doing quite well as far as royalty payments were concerned, and, at the time, had established me as a force to be reckoned with in the horror genre.

But, as always, within the vast and unpredictable world of publishing, my sales eventually tapered off, and my fifteen minutes of fame had passed me by.

But, not before I enjoyed being recognized for all of my hard work.

Just like I feel right now; proud of my past accomplishments, and all of the lessons it taught me along the way, that led me to where I am today.

Lesson learned; *NEVER GIVE UP*.

Always hang tough.

Always fight the good fight, no matter what life tosses your way.

Keep the faith.

Thank God, every single day, for what you *do* have, and not be concerned with what you *don't* have. If it is meant to be, God will let you know soon enough.

Amen.

Part Sixteen

Another day, another round of musings.

Today, I have been thinking about something that I hadn't thought of in what seems like a lifetime now.

The day I was awarded with my GED diploma by Vincennes University.

I had quit highschool in my Junior year, having been more interested in running the streets with my goofy beer drinking buddies and getting into some type of mischief, more often than not.

But by the year 2000, I had begun to realize that I was feeling really guilty, quite embarrassed, actually, that I hadn't taken the time to finish highschool, and had decided to pursue my GED.

Quite a few weeks later, after a lot of hard work and a good dose of tenacity, I did earn my diploma – by the skin of my teeth, as the old saying goes, but I did.

While I was doing so, I also took an IQ test, and to my utter surprise, I had an IQ score of 127.

Which also brings to mind, why would as person with such a high IQ score, *waste* so much of their life as though they had no common sense at all?

That's a good question – which deserves a good answer.

Yet, I can't, for the life of me, come up with any plausible answer.

Just like there is no real plausible answer as to why these damn chemo side effects seem to hang on for dear life – while totally draining mine.

It never fails; each and every time I think I'm starting to feel better, some form of unpleasant side effect kicks in, making me miserable all over again.

I spent four months of my life writing a book about my battle with cancer – and ended the book on a positive note – but now, I'm beginning to wonder if I jumped the gun on that one.

But, as usual, I try my best to hang in there, and, at the same time, look back on a more pleasant time in my life.

My childhood.

Part Seventeen

Today, I woke up thinking about my childhood, when I was around eight years old, when I used to play with my friends at the neighborhood park.

Lester Square park has always been a hot spot for the neighborhood kids, as far back as I can remember. It had a pair of slides – one small one and one quite a bit larger – as well as swing sets, a merry-go-round, a sandbox, a small ball park, and, as of 2007, an enclosed skateboard park that has proved to be quite popular.

When I was a kid, though, the most popular attraction was what I referred to as the "butt-burner" slide.

It was the biggest, tallest slide I'd ever seen at the time, and standing below the wrought iron steps, looking upward, it was like you were a dwarf staring up at the home of a giant.

But the surface of the slide itself was the most intimidating part of it all; long and shiny, so shiny, in fact, you could almost see your reflection in it.

But when you rode that slide, the last thing on your mind was your reflection, more than it was your butt being on fire.

That slick, shiny surface seemed to actually *absorb* the heat from the sun, and if you rode that slide wearing shorts, you might as well have counted on some very sore, chafed buttocks when it was over.

But, at the same time, this unpleasant experience also provided you with the opportunity to act like a real badass, riding that slide and showing off what a tough guy you were when the pretty neighborhood girls would come around to watch you making a fool of yourself.

But to an eight year old, you felt less like a glutton for punishment than you did a real badass hero, so it all worked out in your favor in the end.

I can see it now, sitting at the top of the slide, gazing down upon my loyal spectators, the sun beating down on me, my chest swelling with pride, as I ride that butt burner, the other kids clapping and cheering as I reach the bottom of the slide, my buttocks on fire but my pride still intact, my face beaming.

Ah yes...the *good old days*.

Little did I know at the time, even an act as simple as riding a big slide would someday, at just the right time, would help to bring me out of a deep depression.

Now, as I slowly open my eyes and look out my office door, at the gloomy, cloudy day, it doesn't all seem so sad and hopeless now.

For *now*, that is.

Who knows what tomorrow may bring?

Part Eighteen

Today is no different.

Well, the sun is shining, but other than that, I can't really find anything else positive to speak of.

I also know that's partially my own fault, so I must find a way to bring myself out of another slump, so...I close my eyes and let my mind wander...

#

Yes, more musings.

Today, my mind drifts back to my youth again, when I was in gradeschool.

My best friend, Philip, and I, are riding our bikes around the neighborhood, trying to find some mischief to get into. Back then, though, our mischeif was harmless compared to what sort of mischief today's youth tends to find amusing.

As we ride, we both daydream, and tell each other about our dreams.

Philip: *So, big guy. What's on the agenda for today?*

Me: *How about we ride down to the Memorial and hop a train?*

{We used to ride down to the George Rogers Clark Memorial park, where they still had operative train tracks back then, and hop on one of the train cars and ride it for a few blocks, then jump off.}

    Philip: *Sounds cool to me. Let's go for it.*
    Me: *Let's go!*

Afterward, we would sit on the river wall, smoking cigarettes Philip had liberated from his father's stash, and chat about whatever came to mind.

    Philip: *So, now what?*
    Me: *I don't know. Wait...how about we ride down to the old glass factory, and goof off for a while?*
    Philip: *Cool, we can pretend like we are on the bridge of the Starship Enterprise. I'll be the Captain, and you can be Mr Spock.*
    Me: *Cool, let's go!*

The *Star Trek* TV show wasn't the only thing we were fanatical about. We had been close friends since we were six years old, and always relished the time we spent together.

He, too, sadly passed away in 2022, from a heart attack. I hadn't seen him in over a year, and it was more than heart breaking.

I still haven't gotten over his passing – don't imagine I ever will – and still think about that last day I saw him, his own body still betraying him, but Philip just shrugging it off as easily as he would swat an annoying fly.

That day, when seeing how his body had betrayed him as well, and how such a strong man, not only physically but also in heart and soul, was still capable of a warm smile, a firm handshake, or a big hug when someone would need it, yet ended up this way, it didn't seem quite fair.

He didn't allow his health problems to slow him down or keep him locked up 24-7 or lose his love for others or his sense of humor or anything else that made him who he was. He fought the good fight until the day the good Lord took him home.

He was not only a good friend to me, he was in *inspiration*.

So, I am going to try to be just like he was when he was battling his own health condition, and fight the good fight until the Lord calls me home too.

NEVER GIVE UP.

Don't worry, Philip. I won't give up.

Amen.

Part Nineteen

Musings.
Reflections.
Memories.
They come to me almost every day now, like a DVD of my life, playing on rewind, then on fast forward, and back again.

But the musings are always a *pivotal* time in my life, times that will help me cope with the future.

Today, of all things to think about, my ex-wife comes to mind.

My failed marriage to my ex-wife, Sherri, was most definitely not something I would normally think about, but, here she was, in all her glory, invading my thoughts and day dreams.

Not that I still have anything personal against her after all of this time – we have been divorced since 1989 – but, my time with her, now that I look back on it, is something that would most definitely help me cope with the future.

#

I've noticed that almost *all* of my recent musings have helped me in one way or another, and the memories of my time with Sherri are no different.

We had sort of a "whirlwind" romance, and were already married within six months of dating. I was *really* in love this time, but unfortunately, Sherri didn't share the same feelings.

To make a long story short, we had been in an argument over nothing all that important, when she had decicded to walk out, and ended up never looking back.

After several weeks of not hearing from her, I called her mother's house again to find out she still hadn't seen her either, and she was worried sick.

Fast forward one week.

An old friend of mine, George, dropped by one night, to inform me that he'd seen Sherri at a local night club, dancing and drinking the night away with a man who seemed like he meant much more to her than just a "friend."

Needless to say, I filed for divorce the next day.

#

Point being, you would think that an experience like that would not only sour me on the idea of marriage any time soon again, but also just break my heart in two.

But not me.

I mean, at the time, I was definitely heartbroken at the time, sure, but it hadn't taken me long to realize that an unfaithful, disrespectful, self centered wife who thought no more of me than to have an affair behind my back, wasn't worth all of the tears I shed at the time.

My feelings quickly changed from heartbreak to anger, then to forgiveness, and I moved on.

Point being, never allow affairs of the heart – which can tend to be the most traumatic of all – to make you lose your own love for your fellow man – or, in my case, your fellow woman.

Within Sherri's cruel actions, I found myself all over again, the man I *used* to be, the man I am becoming again right now.

The *good* me.

The *strong* me, the man who had been through hell and back and came out the other end a better man for it.

Amen.

Part Twenty

Today was the same as any other day.

More *musings*.

As usual, they come to me almost every day now, like a DVD of my life, playing on rewind, then on fast forward, and back again.

This time, it was in the form of my old nemesis – and bully – a fellow named Donny.

#

Donny was the neighborhood bully way back when, and I was the perfect target for him; in gradeschool, I was more of the studious, book worm type, made good grades, and knew absolutely nothing about having to use my fists to protect myself.

Perfect target.

That is, until I was in Jr highschool.

By the time I was in eighth grade, I was much taller, bigger in stature, and sick and tired of black eyes and bloody noses and the humility and embarrassment of getting beat up by Donny in front of my friends.

That's when my best friend from gradeschool, Philip, stepped in, and gave me the following advice:

If you don't stand up to him at least ONE time, he will ALWAYS be waiting for you somewhere. It will NEVER end. What you have to do is, let him have the first punch. Then, you haul off and punch right in the NOSE. His eyes will water and his nose will bleed and he will be on his knees.

To make a long story short, I ended up with a black eye, but, he ended up with a fat lip, a loose tooth, and a bloody nose.

He never picked on me again.

After I punched him, just like Phil said, he was on his knees, his nose all swollen and bloody and tears streaming from his eyes. As I raised my fist to hit him again, well...I couldn't bring myself to do it.

As I looked down upon him with his bloody face and tear filled eyes, looking so...beaten, *defeated* – and in front of all his friends – I had decided it was enough. I had proved my point. I was no longer a pushover to be messed with.

And, I felt *sorry* for him.

Looking down on him, I saw *myself* – and couldn't bring myself to inflict any more pain, embarrassment, or humiliation upon him than I already had.

#

Point being, that day – and Donny – both taught me about forgiveness and compassion again.

That day taught me more about the "human condition" than any other day had for a long time, and that memory is still with me today, always reminding me how much more important forgiveness is than revenge.

Once again, it made me a better man.

About thirty years later, I ran into him at Cash N Dash one day. I was buying some chicken and he was buying some cigarettes and lottery tickets. Eyeballing the lotto tickets, I jokingly asked him if he was feeling lucky. He forced a smile and said, no, not really. Then he proceeded to tell me he had just found out he was dying from kidney failure, and his luck had finally run out.

As we parted ways, we shook hands – for the first and last time in our lives – and as he walked out the door, I felt a pang of guilt for punching him so long ago, and wished then that I hadn't been so hell-bent on revenge back then for what he'd done to me as a snot-nosed kid.

A few weeks later he died.

Part Twenty One

And to think that if I hadn't taken the advice of my best friend, Philip, that day, I would have never realized where I was going wrong. I sincerely believe that he knew me well enough – knew my heart and soul well enough – to know I'd end up becoming a better man for my actions that day, and he had initiated the situation on purpose.

That's just what best friends do.

#

As the years went on, at times seeming to pass by me like a blur – just like right now – I experienced even more eye opening, heart wrenching, faith testing situations than I ever had before.

Like it was *meant* to be.

Looking back on all of it now, I truly believe it *was* meant to be. Yet another of God's tests for me, which I passed with flying colors.

Made me who I am today.

I hope it's enough to get me through my battle with the Big C.

Amen.

#

Speaking of which, my constant companion, Mr chemo, is working on me again today.

He is with me almost every day, reminding me of just how much he is in control, and always will be.

But, what he doesn't know yet is, that I am a better man now, a stronger man, and always will be.

Come on, Mr chemo.

Come on, Mr C.

Give it your best shot.

I'm ready.

Part Twenty Two

I woke up to another sunny day today.

I'm glad.

It's really amazing how that, depending on the current weather forecast, can affect your mood for the rest of the day.

If it's cloudy and gloomy, I tend to feel down in the dumps. If the sun is out, I feel like I've been *reborn*, like the sunny day has healed me, and chased the cancer away.

Just wishful thinking, I know, but if it makes me feel better for now, why not? I can always use some pleasant thoughts...

My first kiss.

My first pair of blue jeans.

My first bike.

Well, you get the idea.

Why not? It may be just the musings of a man who feels like he has nothing left to lose, but if it makes me feel better, even if only briefly, why not?

Amen.

#

One of my fondest musings from my childhood was the day I got my brand new bike.

At the age of 11-years-old, I was gifted with my first Stingray bike.

Mom and Dad had felt sorry for me for being tormented by the other neighborhood kids for going through the humiliation of being seen riding an "old folks bike" {code word for the Sunbeam's men's bike, or, worse yet, the dreaded Ladies Triumph 3 bike, which unfortunately some parents considered a "unisex" bike} and had decided to buy me a brand new Stingray bike from Sears and Roebuck.

I was so proud of that bike I would ride it everyday in the Summer, Spring, and Fall, and in the Winter, I would clean it up until it was nice and shiny and immaculately detailed, then store it in the shed out back – which was secured with a sturdy padlock, of course.

I felt like Evil Knievel on my Spyder bike. I would ride it real fast and jump over cracks in the sidewalk and pop wheelies and generally just be *COOL* on my Spyder bike. I would sit on my bike and close my eyes and pretend I was Evil Knievel and I was getting ready to jump over a pit of rattlesnakes or a row of trucks or a pit of fire on my super cool Spyder bike, while a crowd of pretty young girls cheered me on and fell in love with me for my talent and bravery – as well as my natural good looks, of course. Haha.

One thing I *really* loved to do on my Spyder bike was chase the mosquito trucks. Each night around dusk, when the trucks came out, spewing their foul-smelling fog into the air, I'd be right behind them, on my Spyder bike {wearing a pair of sunglasses and a handkerchief over my face, of course} chasing them around the neighborhood.

The reason for chasing a smelly mosquito truck? None, really. An 11-year-old kid doesn't *need* a valid reason to do so. It was just fun to do it on my new bike!

I felt *invincible* on my Spyder bike. I felt...*free*.

To an 11-year-old, a new bike is like a new car would be to a 16-year-old who just obtained their driver's license.

It meant *freedom*.

The freedom to *escape* my own little world for a few minutes. Escape from my lonely little bedroom with the lumpy, twin size bed, the cheap little record player with one busted speaker, or the little cedar chest whre I would hide my alcohol stash.

That's what it was all about, man.

Freedom from my own lonely *mind*.

But, the feeling of pure euphoria I felt from riding my bike, like all things in one's youth, only lasts for so long.

After that first Spring and Summer of enjoying that new found freedom, I had slowly but surely drifted right back to my old life, my old routine. Which taught me yet another valuable life lesson.

No gift, no amount of freedom, will ever help you escape the *reality* of your own sad situation, at least not for long.

Reality is *real*, and escape is just a *fantasy*.

After I realized that, my life slowly but surely began to improve, at least temporarily.

Decades later, it taught me the reality of my situation with the Big C.

Face it up to it, fight the good fight, and move on.

Amen to that, *and* to my new Spyder bike – wherever you are.

Part Twenty Three

It's a sunny day again today, and that's a good thing.

These days, I need all the sunny days I can get. Mr chemo coming to visit again doesn't seem all that bad, when I can walk outside and see the sun and the blue sky and the birds singing, etc.

Today, as I sit at my computer typing away again, my mind drifts back to another pivotal time in my life, the day I decided to stop drinking.

It was in January of 2007.

I had been standing in front of the bathroom mirror, looking at my ghostly reflection, the pale skin and bloodshot eyes and feeling like my whole body was coming apart from the inside out.

As I stood looking into my own eyes – they say that the eyes are the key to the soul – I could see...well, nothing, really.

Just sad, empty eyes, with no life left in them.

Then a little voice in my head – whom I sincerely believe was God speaking to me – began asking me questions:

Do you like the way you look? You're looking pretty rough. I bet you feel even worse. So...do you REALLY want to drink yourself to death? Is your life that worthless to you?

Do you really want to DIE?

NO! Came my reply. *I don't want to die!*

The voice again. *Then wake up and start living instead of DYING.*

I will, I promise! I said.

So that's what I did.

#

Cold turkey, too.

No doctors, no drugs, no therapy.

Just my own will and determination – and with God's will and love for me, of course.

I have now been sober for seventeen years and counting.

That's another reason I am still here; by God's will and love for me, and my own will and strength he so graciously gave me upon my birth.

I just didn't know that until recently.

But I do *now*.

Amen.

Part Twenty Four

It's no wonder I'm so tapped out of energy.

I wake up every day with my body so racked with pain and discomfort, my mind swirling with ghastly visions of what Mr chemo might do to me next, and, on top of that, the constant flood of musings, reflections, of my past – and my future – and where that may lead me I may never know.

But one thing is for sure; I'll be going through it all with *God* on my side.

A lot of folks out there, sadly enough, don't even realize just how close God is sometimes. He is always watching over all of us, we just can't see him. But he *IS* there.

Unless you haven't noticed yet, I, myself, am a prime example of his existence. How else can you explain my *own* existence?

THINK about it.

#

Like I do *every day*.

My entire existence these days is *thinking* about *something*.

Whether it be good or bad or in between, my tired man is always flooded with my own musings, and the only way I can escape them is to fall asleep.

Even then, as I enter the dark, quiet place known as slumber, I tend to dream more than sleep, and wake up wanting to go back to sleep, but knowing that if I do, it will just stockpile even more musings on my weak mind and body, and I won't have the will left any more to fight it.

Then again, why would I *want* to fight it? I mean, hasn't it proven to be my life line to normalcy? My salvation from the past, that will someday be my salvation for the future?

See what I mean?

But God willing, I'll make it through.

#

Today, as I sit at my old PC, typing away, my tired mind drifts back to yet another time when I was happy for a change, but then the *musings* came flooding back in again, and my good mood seemed to vanish in a puff of smoke.

Like magic.

But there were no magic tricks involved; only my own sad existence.

Today, the flood is yet another mish-mosh of numerous "musings," like there is a tiny DVD player inside of my head, being played on rewind and fast forward and back again.

So jumbled up are these musings, that I can't even focus on any certain one, making my mind race even more, making me even more confused.

Then I close my eyes, take several deep breaths, and try to clear my head – and I *pray.*

When I open my eyes, I'm still here, sitting at my PC and typing away, but no longer so confused or tired.

You see? God is *still* with me – and always will be, through the good and the bad and in between.

He will be there at the end of this journey, waiting for me, cancer or no cancer involved.

As a matter of fact, I think at times that he actually encourages my memories, my musings, in order to let me see just *WHY* I'm still here.

I guess I'll know soon enough.

Part Twenty Five

Here I am, back again.

Today, I woke up thinking about something I hadn't thought about for quite some time – had tried to block it out, in all honesty.

My father's funeral.

#

Yeah...I know.

Sounds sort of cold hearted, doesn't it?

I didn't mean to sound that way.

It's just that I have always felt guilty about the day we laid my father to rest, because we hadn't been very close for the last few years before his death.

Allow me to explain.

My father exuded an air of almost overbearing authority, ran the house with an iron hand, and his idea of parental responsibility was siring me, feeding me, making sure I did my homework and my chores.

He wasn't necessarily cruel to me, but he wasn't necessarily kind to me, either. I was just there, for better or for worse, and we didn't really spend a lot of time together as I grew up.

I didn't realize until much later, *why* he was such a strict and quiet type. But after I did, I had also realized why I grew up being such a true survivor.

#

It wasn't until *after* my father's funeral, that I had realized why he'd been so tough on me at times.

He had wanted me to be a *real* man, one with a good work ethic and morals, just like his own generation had grown up.

The last *great* generation, before my own great generation, the baby boomers.

But at the time, just being a reclusive, snot-nosed little kid, I hadn't paid much attention to his real intentions.

His *good* intentions.

But the day after his funeral, it had hit me hard. I spent the day putting two and two together, and had realized that I'd spent all of those years helping my mother take care of him after he had a bad stroke, and hadn't learned anything of any importance until *after* he had passed away.

When it was too late to say a nice, heartfelt goodbye to the man who made me what I am today.

But I now know why.

It's never too late to say I'm sorry, or make amends or make up for lost time.

So...thank you dad, for making me a *real* man, a *true* survivor.

Amen.

Part Twenty Six

It's another sunny day, and I'm glad.

After yesterday, I don't think I could stand another gloomy day. I've had enough gloom and doom days over the last five months to last a lifetime.

But the *musings*....they just keep on coming.

I'm sure they always will, too. At least until the day I die, whenever that may be.

If so? So be it. I'd rather die a better man for it than not.

Just not right now.

#

I have so many "musings" to sort through first.

Just like the one I'm thinking about today; my time in jail and prison.

Long story short, I had allowed my drinking to get the best of me, had ended up in jail over a probation violation, and then, due to jail overcrowding, was shipped off to prison for five months.

Needless to say, I had definitely learned to be a true survivor in prison. If not, a person can end up a target for the wolves.

You meet a lot of interesting characters in prison, too. For example, Mr Herb Proctor.

Herb was a vicious, violent child molester, who, upon being arrested for his long list of atrocities, had proceeded to *bite* one of the arresting officers, and ripping a small chunk of flesh right out of the officer's right forearm.

Needless to say, Herb had a very violent and unhealthy appetite.

Point of the story being, if spending some not so quality time around men like Herb won't make you a real man, *nothing* will. In prison, you learn really fast to either "man up," and guard your own ass and have eyes in the back of your head, or end up being on the recieving end of hell on Earth.

I, myself, learned this fact quickly, and kept my mouth shut, my head down, and my mind and wits wired tight.

Five months later, I walked out of prison a free man, and the better for having paid my dues to society and walking a straight line.

Just like I am right now – my father didn't raise a punk, you know.

Amen.

Part Twenty Seven

Musings.

Reflections.

Memories.

Soul searching.

Call it what you want, but I've been doing a lot of it lately.

#

Another day, another musing or two.

But today, my mind isn't so muddled and I feel like I have at least a modicum of energy to work with.

The musings are *slowing down*, and I think that's a good thing. Or at least I hope it is.

Today, my mind drifted back to the years I spent taking care of Mom after she broke her hip.

Unfortunately, I am no stranger to the subjects of pain, suffering, sickness, and death.

Over the last 25 years, I have said goodbye to countless old friends who have passed on way too young. I have been a pallbearer for several of them. I have found a dead body in a motel room {I worked there at the time as a maintenance man} and I spent almost five years watching my own Father sit in a chair and slowly wither away until he mercifully passed on.

One would think that these experiences would toughen me up, *harden* me to the subject of death. Not so. All it did for me was to make me feel sick, empty, and depressed. Does being around death and sadness make you a tough guy? Not really. Far from it, actually.

And it hasn't gotten any easier with time.

Then, in 2013, my Mom fell and broke her hip.

#

It had only been about two years since my Father's passing, and Mom was, as usual, hanging in there.

She was tough, resilient almost, when it came to his death. She had been married to him for over 60 years, and she missed him dearly. I used to watch her sit in front of the TV set and glance back and forth toward the recliner he used to sit in, wishing she could still see him there – even if it did mean going through the grueling, back breaking process of taking care of him all over again.

I didn't know then what I know now, how hard it had been for her.

But life went on that way, Mom alone and wishing things could be different, and then, one day in September of 2013, her life did change drastically – but not for the better.

She had been in the kitchen washing dishes, and I had just walked outside long enough to take out the trash, maybe 90 seconds. When I came back inside, I found her lying on the kitchen floor, on her back, her eyes filled with tears and her whole body shaking.

Surprisingly, she was calm. She said she had fallen down and was experiencing the worst pain she'd ever felt in her entire life. My first thought at her age was she'd broken her hip or pelvis. It was the hip.

I knelt down and held her hand and told her it was going to be OK, I would call 911. A few minutes later the ambulance came and took her over to GSH and the prognosis was bad; she would have to have a total hip replacement.

Thus began my journey into being an in-home caregiver for her for the next 6 years.

And I would do it all again.

Bad things happen to good people.

Tell me about it.

I had begun to feel bitter and hateful. *Why is a good woman like my mama suffering this way?! This is NOT fair!*

But no matter how much I would walk outside and gaze up at the Heavens above and scream these questions, I didn't receive any real answer.

Or at least I thought so back then.

God's plan for my mom – and for me – hadn't come full circle yet.

And when it did, the answers to my questions had been there all along.

Part Twenty Eight

When bad things began happening to my Mom, it was a vivid reminder of what a pessimist I'd been for a long time.

As comedian Charle Chaplin once said, "In the end, everything is just a gag." He apparently was an optimist by nature. But me?

Not so. I'd always had alot of trouble finding a silver lining in every cloud, or a pot of gold at the end of every rainbow. In other words, I may have *read* fiction, or *watched* it on the screen, but, I didn't *live it.* I tried my best to remain in a virtual state of reality, no matter how hard times were to deal with.

Thus my habit of becoming a recluse; to escape my own sad reality.

But as of 2013 onward, my reclusive habits were a thing of the past.

#

As it turned out – for me and mom both – it was a blessing more than a curse.

Gone were my days as a recluse, yes, but at the same time, my life was enriched beyond belief, as was my mom's life too.

During those six years, my mom and I had become closer than we'd ever been before. We spent those years becoming reacquainted again, and by the time she left us to be placed in a nursing home, my heart was literally broken in two at the thought of not being able to take care of her anymore.

I felt heartbroken and I felt guilty.

But most of all, I felt all *alone* again, and knew deep down in my heart that I would never be the same again.

Then, in 2022, my brother and I received the call we had been dreading, but knew we would hear eventually.

Mom had passed away, in her sleep, at the age of ninety one years old.

I can honestly part of me died with her.

But as time went on once again, I had slowly but surely realized that taking care of my mom all that time had also been part of God's plan for me, and I had done an admirable job of doing so.

Something my mom said to me just a few months before she went into the nursing home comes to mind today, which shows me that my mom knew all along that God had a plan for me, too.

She said, "I hope you know that I have *always* loved you. You are tough and strong and you have helped me *SO* much. You're going to be just fine, and I hope you know that now."

Looking back on that day now, how could I ever feel as though I'm not tough enough to beat this cancer?

I guess we'll see, won't we?

Part Twenty Nine

Today is another sunny day, and in all honesty, I believe it was meant to be that way.

I believe God himself intervened, knowing that I, myself – as well as plenty of other folks out there – really needed a sunny day, so we have one.

We are all just human, and we all need something to brighten up the day now and then. Today was one of those days.

As I sit here at my PC typing away again, I am thinking of nothing in particular this time. I think that my "musings" are finally beginning to taper off, and to be honest, that makes me feel sad.

Not depressed, mind you, just sort of sad in the way that I will miss the musings – the memories – now.

After all, they did help me understand just how strong I really am, and where my future may lead me now.

If I do succumb to this cancer, at least I'll be able to say that I gave it my best fight, and was brave in the face of extreme adversity.

Always keep the faith.

Always fight the good fight.

Even if you lose, you won't really be a loser.

Amen.

Part Thirty

I woke up to another sunny day today.

But I have no musings to speak of.

And that's okay, because I sincerely believe that most of my important musings – the most pivotal times in my life – have already been shown to me, and all that's left now is to carry on with the future.

I know now how my life will end; I will beat cancer and live for a while, or it will beat me, and I will die.

But, nobody will ever be able to say that I didn't live a long, interesting life, and became a better man for it in the end.

To be completely honest, though, I hope I live for a while longer. I would like to enjoy a few more beautiful sunsets, and listen to the birds singing and the crocketys chirping and bathe in the Earthly light that God has so graciously blessed me with.

Just a little while longer, okay Lord?

I guess I'll find out soon enough.

The author

David Boyer is a Christian, a multi-genre writer, a true crime buff, and the author of several coming of age novellas, numerous horror and scifi stories, as well as the author of numerous essays including the subjects of government corruption, Christianity, bullying, and cyber-stalking.

He lives in Vincennes, Indiana, with his cat, Holly Jean, who now serves as his copy editor by jumping on the computer keyboard when he's not looking.

Books: {Non-fiction}
True crime:
Small Town Murder: True Crime Stories From Knox County, Indiana
Murder In the Hoosier Heartland: Infamous Indiana Murderers & Fledgling Serial Killers
Murder & Mayhem In the Hoosier Heartland: Mysterious Disappearances & Bizarre Murders In Indiana
The Blitz: A Rape Victim's Story
Vanished In Vincennes: the Mysterious Disappearance and Death Of Dolores Oliver
47 Years of Hell: The Dolores Oliver Murder: Still Unsolved
Small Town Murder In Knox County, Indiana: Hate Crimes, Witch Hunts, and A Definitive List of Indiana Serial Killers
The Guy In The Blue Shirt

Non-fiction: {paranormal, bio & memoir}
Haunted Heartland: Haunted Hoosiers Tell Their Ghost Stories
Strange Happenings In the Hoosier Heartland
I Remember When, In Vincennes...Volume 1
Growing Up In Vincennes – Volumes 2 – 5
The Time of Our Lives: Growing Up Cool In Vincennes, Indiana

Essays:
Bullying: the Road to Recovery and Forgiveness
Privacy In the Age of the Internet: How Sexting and Sharing Private Photos Can lead To Cyber-Stalking
Once An Alcoholic, Always An Alcoholic? The Cold

Hard Truth About Our Addictions
Travesties of Jutice: Flaws In Our Legal System That Imprison the Innocent
Will the REAL Christian Please Stand Up?
Racism in the 21st Century: ALL Lives Matter
Conflicted Souls: How the Man In Black Saved My Life
Crossing the Rainbow Bridge: Saying Goodbye To Our Beloved Pets

Books: {Fiction}
Mystery, Indiana
Human Sawdust
Mutant Moon and Other Stories
Lucid Nightmares – A Collection of Short Fiction
The World According To Luther Biggs

Stories: {Long fiction, novellas}
Mystery, Indiana
The Mind of Luther Biggs
LUTHER
Jenny
Lester Talbot and His Magic Eye
Beautiful Ghosts
Pretty Flamingo
Jack and Norma Jean
The Things We Leave Behind – Volumes 1 – 3
Ghosts of Summer
Gardens
Claustrophobia
The Cemetery Artist
Brain Pie
Beast
The Jailhouse Movie Star

Easy Pickings
The Dominant Thumb
Joyride
The Maverick
Freak
Grandma's Gooseberry Pie
Dancing With the King
Always In My Heart
Hillbilly Moonshine Zombies
Home
Sheva
A Debt Repaid In Full
The Enlightening Darkness
The Good Neighbor
Wander
The Hungry Ones
A Gunfighter's Legacy
Dead Man's Hand
Inhuman Experiments – Part 1, 2, and 3
Jennifer
Spider Bait
Poor Larry
Creepy Crawl
They Call Me The Wolf
Welcome To Deadman's Gulch
Uncle Marty
The Guy In The Blue Shirt
Mutant Moon
Elnora's Eyes
Goodnight, My Love
Wildflowers
Blue Moonlight
Black Midnight

Two Men, Sitting On The Front Porch, Talking About
The End Of the World
True Love Never Dies: An Apocalyptic Love Story
Save Me
Shadow Dolls
The Ghosts Of Halloween
Restless Hearts
The King Of Pain

Other recent book releases by David Boyer
{Now available on Lulu.com}

Dolores Oliver, fondly nick-named 'Lert' by her friends as a term of endearment, was out an out-going and friendly woman who was well liked by all who knew her.

Yet, on September 7, 1974, while on a visit to a local bar to chat with friends, she simply vanished without a trace. Foul play was immediately suspected by her family, who knew in their hearts that they could think of absolutely no one who would want to do her any harm.

Yet her lifeless body was found at the end of October in a bean field by a farmer in Illinois. Lawrence County coroner Dale Nichols was able to make a positive ID through dental records and a ring Mrs Oliver was wearing.

Who would have done such a thing, and why? Hopefully, VANISHED IN VINCENNES will help to finally solve one of the oldest cold cases in Indiana, and bring her family some closure they have sought for so long.

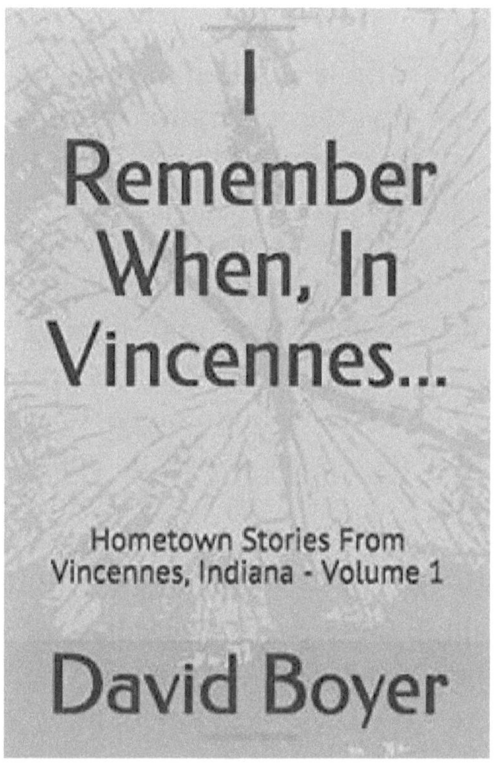

Unfortunately, even small towns – Vincennes included – eventually change, sometimes for the better, and other times, not so much. It's the natural order of things.

Trees grow old and fall. Sidewalks split and crack and are replaced for public safety's sake. Old houses – and all the memories associated with them – are demolished and replaced with parking lots or duplexes. Even historical landmarks, Mother Nature and Father Time having taken their toll, sadly, vanish – except for our own pictures and memories of them.

Luckily for Vincennes residents, local historian Norbert Brown has created a Facebook group page entitled, *Vincennes Remember When,* to help all of us keep our fond memories intact, and to reminisce and enjoy them 24-7.

It was his infinite wisdom of our local history and group page that was the inspiration for this book – and the stories within. Some of these stories may elicit a tear, some laughter.

Some may remind you of an old friend you haven't seen since high school – or, sadly, one that has passed in recent years. Some may remind you of your childhood, your teenage years – or having to bid them farewell, in order to move on to bigger and better things; marriage, children, grandchildren, and a lifetime of wonderful memories that only a tight-knit, loving family can provide.

It is my sincere belief that there will be a story for *everybody* within these pages, regardless of whether you may be a Vincennes history buff or not.

As of 2015, it is believed that there are at least 200 serial killers active in the United States at any given time.

33 of them were from Indiana.

Nobody in their own home town would have wanted to imagine a fledgling {or full fledged} serial killer lurking about, searching for his next victim. Or imagine one being their next door neighbor or the relative of a friend or even attending the local college.

Yet, since the early 1970s, Vincennes, Indiana, Knox County, and Indiana in general has had it's share of cold blooded murder.

It's really sad – as well as terrifying – to even imagine all these brutal, cold blooded murders have taken place in small town communities, where, at one time, we could all trust just about everyone we met at least to the extent they'd do us no harm; a time when could leave our doors unlocked at night or a window open for a cool breeze or not have to worry about where our children were – or if they'd ever come home again.

In SMALL TOWN MURDER, we will be examining local cases, old cases, more recent cases, and the aftermath it leaves behind for the victim's families – as well as taking an in-depth look into a deep, dark, world none of us would ever want to see – but has been here all along, and, most likely, always will be.

Bonus:
Excerpts from the book
Reflections On My Own Mortality
By David Boyer

ONE

It's really ironic, isn't it, how we spend our youth tossing caution to the wind at every turn, believing we will live forever?

I know I did.

I think we all do, when we are growing up. I grew up in the baby boomer generation, for example, and the only cares we had was going to school, riding our bikes around the neighborhood until dark, going home to eat dinner at the family table, then TV and bedtime.

Then, on weekends, we'd be up early, eating a bowl of cereal and watching Saturday morning cartoons, then out to meet up with our friends for a long day of creating new adventures, and some more great memories, of course.

We all unknowingly took it all for granted, never having any inclination that we'd grow older by the day, month, and year. Graduating from highschool, getting a job, starting a family.

Growing up.

The whole time, as we moved on, growing older and hopefully wiser and happier, never having any idea that someday, whether it be a few years from now or decades from now, we would eventually have to face our own mortality.

In my case, it was in the form of a cancer, that invaded my lymphnodes, and moved on to my chest.

It's funny – well, ironic, that is – how your own

mortality tends to show you just how *vulnerable* you really are, and at a time when you thought that your life was going pretty well, despite your other recent disappointments – and heartaches.

When the old grim reaper came to visit me – in the form of squamous cell carcinoma – I had just gone through the death my beloved cat, Toby, my best friend friend from gradeschool, Phil, and my mother, who had spent the last two years in a nursing home until she had mercifully passed away in her sleep.

My mind, heart, and soul had already been torn asunder, and I was just barely getting back into the swing of things when my body began to betray me in the form of the "Big C."

#

I had begun with a simple sore throat and a cough, with the cough being a bit more persistent than the soreness in my throat. In the past, these symptoms, for me, had been merely signs my sinus trouble was flaring up because of a change in the weather, so I simply purchased some over the counter medicine and thought no more of it.

A few weeks later, my cough had subsided, but my sore throat was becoming almost unbearable.

Then one night, as I stood in front of the bathroom mirror brushing my teeth, I saw it; a very small but visible lump under my tongue, and a small but visible lump on the right side of my throat.

I knew then that sinus trouble was going to be the least of my worries in the future.

TWO

Over the next few weeks, I spent countless bours at the doctor's office or the hospital, undergoing countless tests and exams and being poked and prodded and given certain medications and having x-rays and pet scans, and well...you name it, I had been subjected to it.

Now, bear in mind, this was during the same time I had just been diagnosed with an enlarged prostate, high blood pressure, as well as cataracts in both eyes, so the thought of possibly having cancer wasn't exactly what someone in my shoes wanted to deal with.

Then, of all things that could have happened to me, the pain intensified.

#

I don't know if you have ever experienced the degree of pain that swollen, cancerous lymphnodes can produce, but if not, I hope and pray you *never* have to go through this. I wouldn't wish this kind of pain and discomfort on my worst enemy – that is, if I had one. These days, I do my best to let bygones be just that, in the past, and love more than hate.

I thought I'd felt extreme pain in the past, but there was absolutely *no* comparison.

I'd had my left thumb crushed off at work and grafted back on, had twenty-eight teeth pulled {a lot of them having been infected} had a broken nose, black eyes, kicked in the groin, I mean...I had experienced all sorts of pain, but nothing like the pain I experienced with what I not so fondly refer to as "The Big C."

#

It began slowly, like a nocturnal predator slithering through the darkness, sneaking up on me, bit by bit, just a little worse each day, until the day that over the counter pain relievers no longer had any effect at all, except for providing me with acid reflux and an upset stomach.

By that time, the pain in my throat was so extreme, I couldn't eat or drink anything without being in pain. My diet began to change, and rapid weight loss followed, to add insult to injury.

My doctor quickly prescribed some very powerful pain meds he referred to as "Norco," and since then, at least I have something to combat the pain with at times it becomes too overbearing.

But...then I had the "side effects" of my new medication to deal with; chronic constipation, stomach cramps, and acid reflux.

Back to the doctor again!

THREE

Just when I thought I'd seen it all as far as pain or discomfort was concerned, then came the rapid and not so subtle changes in my daily life style.

Where as I had been used to the same sleeping schedule, working on my computer each day at a certain time, eating at a certain time, etc.

But not after the Big C had grabbed ahold of me and turned my life upside down.

#

One thing about the Big C, it isn't prejudice. In it's beady little evil eyes, we are *all* equally worthless and subject to extreme bodily pain and psychological torture.

It isn't concerned with skin color or personal background or what Church you attend – or don't bother attending – on Sunday mornings.

All it is concerned with is making your life as miserable {and maybe as short} as possible, and as quickly as possible.

Then there are the *dreams*.

#

Well, more like nightmares, actually.

You combine your current state of health, your daily meds and other supplements, your narcotic pain relievers, and, of course, your current frame of mind, if you *are* lucky enough to go to sleep, it will be a fitful sleep at best.

My sleep patterns have changed a lot since my diagnosis; instead of falling asleep within a reasonable amount of time, I now lay there wide awake, my mind always racing with ghastly visions of the cancer inside of me, moving around again, the tiny little evil cells coarsing through my bloodstream, attacking everything in sight.

One night, I had a dream that my cancer was actually chasing me, and was catching up to me, when, suddenly, I was whisked away into a bright light up in the clouds, which I'm sure was Heaven.

Then I woke up to the same old thing I always wake up to; sleep deprevation, headache, sour stomach, and fatigue.

I still think it ws Heaven I saw, though. At least I hope it was.

#

That's another thing about cancer you can always depend on; it will test your faith.

I'm not necessarily talking about your faith in God, either. I'm speaking, in general, of one's faith in *themselves*.

In my situation, if you didn't try your best to have faith in *yourself*, to carry on as best you can, no matter what life tossed at you on any given day, you just...*give up*, believe me, you *will die*, and possibly sooner than later.

You have to remain positive. You have to remain calm. You have to do your best to live each and every day as though it may be your last, but, at the same time, you must also keep the *faith*, the faith that God graced you with upon birth, that you *will* make it through all of this someday.

Without your faith, and faith in yourself, you might as well roll back over in the morning and give up.

I, myself, don't intend to do so.

FOUR

It always strikes me as really amusing – but not in a cruel, uncaring way, of course – how tough some guys think they are until the Big C pays them a visit.

I used to think I was a real tough guy, too. I mean, in the way of being gifted with a strong constitution for hard work, and a threshold for pain. I had inherited that from my Father, James, and I was gifted with a good, kind heart from my Mother, Jeanne.

But, you toss cancer into the mix, and even the toughest of guys can end up a blubbering mess.

I remember the day I was told I had cancer. I sat there, taking it all in, pretending to be a tough guy. Then, when I got home, in private, I sat down in my room and cried like a baby with a dirty diaper.

Tough guy...yeah, *right*.

#

But don't worry, guys, it doesn't make you *weak* to break down and cry.

It doesn't make you any less of a man, It doesn't make you appear childish in front of your loved ones. It doesn't make you look like a big baby in front of your friends.

It shows that you have a big heart, a *good* heart, and, last, but not least, it shows that you are man enough to know when you are defeated.

But, what do we do when we are defeated?

We get back up, brush ourselves off, and jump right back into the fight again,

It works the same way with cancer.

You know you have a *very* formidable opponent you're dealing with, and you know you have to fight the toughest fight you've ever fought in your life if you are to survive.

You can do it.

I know.

#

You may wake up in the morning feeling even weaker and more fatigued that the day before. You may look in the bathroom mirror at those weak, bloodshot eyes and pale skin and thinning hair, and wonder how you're going to make it through.

You may fall asleep at night wondering if you will even wake up in the morning. Or if you will wake up feeling even worse.

You may wake up sick at your stomach and weak in the knees and barely make it into the bathroom before voiding your stomach of all or any nutritional content you may have had stored there.

You may find yourself curled up on the floor and crying and wishing it was all over, even if it meant that you just...*gave up*.

I don't think anyone could blame you.

Even God.

But, that means you lost your *faith*, and let yourself down.

When you needed yourself and your strength the most.

So you crawl back to your bed, take a short nap, and while you're lying there, you promise yourself – and God – that the next day, you will *not* let this beat you down.

You are *still* a tough guy.

If you were *not* a tough guy, you wouldn't be so bound and determined to fight the Big C with all your heart and soul now, would you?

Just saying.

FIVE

What has really amazed me about my journey so far, is my own willpower.

You'd really be surprised how the word "cancer" tends to make a guy wake up and smell the roses, so to speak.

I wake up each day, knowing that those nasty little cancer cells are most likely migrating further down South, but still do my level best to enjoy my day.

Dealing with the Big C, a lot of the process is *psychological*, you know. Seriously.

It's in your own personal mindset on certain days. For example, if you wake up feeling really low down? If the weather permits? Take a walk around the neighborhood. Chat with your neighbors.

Literally *stop* and smell the roses.

Stop and pet the neighborhood cats.

Listen to the birdies sing.

Gaze up at the sunshine and fluffy white clouds and be thankful for the opportunity.

Or, just in case you aren't feeling up to any outdoor activities, find something you enjoy doing on the *inside*.

Watch your favorite TV show.

Eat one of your favorite snacks.

Order a pizza and watch a DVD.

Read a good book.

Enjoy one of your favorite hobbies.

If you don't have any particular hobbies, take up a *new* hobby.

You get the idea.

Do *not* allow the Big C to run your life for you; *you* run your *own* life.

Stop, take a deep breath, close your eyes, and use your *willpower* to overcome the moment in a *positive* way. *Positive* thoughts.

You can do it. Believe me, I know.

#

But, if you are having one of these really bad days, and your willpower isn't quite up to par, keep this in mind:

God and Jesus are rooting for you. God's plan for you is not over yet. If this was meant to be your *last* days on this beautiful Earth God created for us, you wouldn't be here to live yet another day.

You *can* do it. Just open your heart to God and keep telling yourself...*I can do this*.

Your journey, just like mine, isn't quite over yet. Keep the faith and *BELIEVE*.

www.ingramcontent.com/pod-product-compliance
Lightning Source LLC
Chambersburg PA
CBHW051901130726
47987CB00002B/937